The Miracles of Jesus

An Introduction

THE MIRACLES OF JESUS

AN INTRODUCTION

Franz Mussner

Translated by

Albert Wimmer

UNIVERSITY OF NOTRE DAME PRESS
NOTRE DAME

NIHIL OBSTAT:
      Joseph Hoffman, C.S.C.,
      Censor Deputatus

IMPRIMATUR:
      ✠Leo A. Pursley, D.D.
      Bishop of Fort Wayne-South Bend
      March 15, 1968

Original German title:

DIE WUNDER JESU: EINE HINFÜHRUNG

First published by Kösel-Verlag KG, Munich, 1967

Biblical quotations are taken from *The Jerusalem Bible* (Doubleday, 1966).

FOREWORD

The free atmosphere around the exegesis of Holy Scripture is at times agitated by storms which can bend trees and even uproot them. This is called demythologizing. The Miracles of Jesus have also found themselves within the storm belt. Are they only images of what Jesus will do after the parousia, or are they historical facts?

It is the task of exegesis to present arguments for the discerning application of demythologizing in order not only to save the historicity of the Miracles of Jesus but also to give a deeper reason for them. That is done in this small book by Franz Mussner. The result of his research is summed up in the sentence "Without the miracles of Jesus there is no Christ."

The author is a highly respected professor of New Testament exegesis at the University of Regensburg in Bavaria. In addition to having written many purely scientific works, a commentary to the Jacobine Epistle and a book on the Johannine view among them, he belongs to the few who may be able to make modern exegesis fruitful for a forward-looking catechetics. Witness to this the new book about the Miracles of Jesus in the same series as his *The Use of Parables in Catechetics.*

JOSEF GOLDBRUNNER

PREFACE

To many, even serious Christians, the miracles of Jesus together with all the other miracles in the Bible have become a problem for whose solution they sincerely struggle. Expert exegetes who have a professional interest in Holy Scripture feel an obligation to come to their aid with all their knowledge and strength, no matter how they, too, and exactly they, are painfully aware of the intricacy of the subject matter. Yet before an individual interpretation of the accounts of Jesus' miracles in the gospels can be furnished, it is absolutely necessary to account first for "the preliminary questions" which accompany the topic "The Miracles of Jesus." For it is only in this manner that we can free ourselves for objective, individual interpretation. This book will deal with these questions.

It is the hope of the author to be able to present, also, individual interpretations at one time or another. They will appear in the same series under the title *The Message of the Miracles of Jesus*.

FRANZ MUSSNER

CONTENTS

Contents

ABBREVIATIONS

BBB	*Bonner Biblische Beiträge*
BZ	*Biblische Zeitschrift*
LThK	*Lexikon für Theologie und Kirche,* ed. by J. Höfer and K. Rahner (Freiburg, 1957–1967)
RGG	*Die Religion in Gegenwart und Geschichte*
TThZ	*Trierer Theologische Zeitschrift*
ThW	*Theologisches Wörterbuch zum Neuen Testament,* ed. by G. Friedrich (Stuttgart, 1933–)
ZKTh	*Zeitschrift für katholische Theologie*
ZNW	*Zeitschrift für die neutestamentliche Wissenschaft und die Kunde der älteren Kirche*

The Miracles of Jesus

An Introduction

I

THE PROBLEM

The topic "The Miracles of Jesus" entails historical, form-critical, and theological questions. The historical investigation deals mainly with whether Jesus of Nazareth worked any miracles at all or whether the accounts of miracles in the gospels are merely post-Easter "entries" in the pre-Easter life of Jesus. Were these accounts occasioned by the "Easter-experience" of the disciples and the formation of an explicit "Christology" in the post-Easter teachings of the early Christian Church, wherein Jesus of Nazareth was made into a divine miracle-worker in close following of other cases from the history of religion?

1

From a form-critical point of view it is the question of whether the accounts of miracles in the gospels, which as such originated from the post-Easter teachings, have been influenced by the post-Easter belief in Christ to such an extent that, if there was an historical occurrence at all, we have no way of taking hold of it anymore. Furthermore, which theological "tendencies" influenced the individual evangelists in their renditions of the miracles, tendencies found already among the synoptics, but particularly in the case of St. John?

Finally, the theological question: What is the kerygmatic significance of the miracles of Jesus and their accounts in the gospels in connection with the historical deeds of Jesus as well as the gospel narratives about his life.

After these introductory thoughts it becomes already quite clear that our topic is most intimately connected with the quest for the "historical" Jesus, a question which is widely and passionately discussed nowadays due to the emphasis placed on the form-critical approach. It goes without saying that a mere "introduction" must be taken as such and cannot be expected to discuss all those questions relating to the topic "The Miracles of Jesus" in minute detail. This book can and shall only point out ways to a possible solution of the problem.[1]

THE HISTORICAL QUESTION

THE UNITY OF WORD AND WORK IN THE DIVINE PLAN OF SALVATION

To limit the saving activity of God in the Bible to the revelation of his word contradicts any penetrating view of the Bible. God reveals himself and works his salvation *through his words and deeds*. Word and deed are certainly not quite the same thing in the saving action of God (even though the Hebrew term *dābār* means "word" as well as "thing"—affair, object)[1]; to reduce the events of revelation and salvation to a mere "revelation in words" would plainly contradict the ideas and the understanding of Holy Scripture. It is

rather significant that we already encounter at the beginning of the Bible a
revealing example, when in the conclusion
of the story of creation (Gn 1:1–2) creation by word ("God said") and creation by
work ("God created") are intimately
linked up with each other.[2] This is obviously a result of the fact that Israel was
deeply convinced that the words and works
of God form a harmonious synthesis.

The parallelism of creation by work and
creation by word prevents "either one of
the two concepts from being made absolute; thereby the operation of God is more
fully realized."[3] Yet, not only word and
work form a unity in the divine acts of
God according to the belief of the Old Testament but creation and salvation as well.
The prayer treasure of the people of Israel
offers a particularly apt illustration of this
in Psalm 146, where it says in verses 5 ff:

> Happy the man who has the God of Jacob
>   to help him,
> whose hope is fixed on Yahweh his God,
> *maker of heaven and earth,*
> and the sea, and all that these hold!

6

Yahweh, forever faithful,
gives justice to those denied it,
gives food to the hungry,
gives liberty to prisoners.

Yahweh restores sight to the blind,
Yahweh straightens the bent,
Yahweh protects the stranger,
he keeps the orphan and widow.

Jahweh loves the virtuous,
and frustrates the wicked.
Yahweh reigns for ever,
your God, Zion, from age to age.

Verse 6 speaks of Yahweh as the maker of heaven and earth. This, then, is followed by an enumeration of the divine works of salvation. In verse 10 everything is subsumed under the concept of "Yahweh's kingship"[4]: The "malkut Yahweh," the βασιλεία τοῦ θεοῦ, the kingship of God, is expressed in the divine works of creation as well as salvation according to Psalm 146.

How much Israel viewed the powerful works of God in creation and salvation as a unity is particularly emphasized in Psalm 145:3 ff:

Can anyone measure the magnificence
of Yahweh the great, and his inexpres-
sible grandeur?

Celebrating your acts of power,
an age shall praise your doings to another.
Oh, the splendour of your glory, your
renown!
I tell myself the story of your marvellous
deeds.

Men will proclaim your fearful power
and I shall assert your greatness;
they will celebrate your generous kindness
and joyfuly acclaim your righteousness.

. . . .

Yahweh, all your creatures thank you,
and your faithful bless you.
Kingly and glorious they proclaim you,
they affirm your might.

Let mankind learn your acts of power,
and the majestic glory of your sover-
eignty!

. . . .

Always true to his *promises*,
Yahweh shows love in all he *does*.

God's "works of power" in his creation and in the plan of salvation are hailed as the manifestations of his universal kingship and as "marvellous deeds," that is, miracles (verse 5) of his kindness and love. Kraus notes in conclusion to this psalm: "Yahweh's kingship is under the sign of faithfulness to his plan of salvation and of his love which reaches down to the needy and the 'bent.' This psalm is an important milestone on the way to the proclamation of the βασιλεία τοῦ θεοῦ in the New Testament."[5] These are exemplary proofs for the conviction of the unity of God's activity in creation and salvation, both *experienced in the form of "miracles."* Israel is daily surprised at the divine works of power in creation; she knows how to praise them (see the so-called creation psalms), and the prophet admonishes Israel: "Did you not know, had you not heard? Was it not told you *from the beginning?* Have you not understood *how the earth was founded?* . . . Lift your eyes and look. Who made these stars if not he who drills them like

an army, calling each one by name?" (Is
40:21,26).

According to Deuteronomy 3:23 Moses
experienced, in the divine works of power,
the greatness of God the Creator during
Israel's exodus: "My Lord Yahweh . . .
you that have begun to reveal your greatness and your power to your servant, you
whose works and mighty deeds no one in
heaven or on earth can rival . . ." (see also
Jer 27:5; 32:17: "Ah, Lord Yahweh, you
have made the heavens and the earth with
your great power and outstretched arm.
To you nothing is impossible.") Throughout her history Israel is constantly confronted by the "strong arm" of God the
Creator! The making of heaven and earth
is the greatest miracle of God according to
the belief of the Old Testament, and
through his works of power throughout
the history of Israel the people recognize
the "name" of their God. "You performed
signs and wonders in the land of Egypt and
do the same today, in Israel and among
mankind. You have won the name that is
yours today" (Jer 32:20). Thus Israel wit-

nesses God the Creator throughout her history as the *God of wonders*.

In nature as well as in the guidance of Israel and the nations of the world to salvation, his power and thus his kingship is revealed.[6] Hebrew thinking does not differentiate with respect to the divine works of power as to "whether they are occurrences in accordance with the laws of nature or whether they represent a breach of those very laws. . . . Every event through which Yahweh reveals his power and greatness is considered a 'wonder' " in the widest sense of the word.[7] Rather illuminating in this respect is Psalm 107, a liturgical song of thanksgiving. Here four groups of "Yahweh's redeemed" appear: (1) wanderers and pilgrims returning from an exhaustive trip through the desert, 4–9; (2) prisoners who were set free, 10–16; (3) persons who recuperated from serious illness, 17–22; (4) sailors who were saved from a storm and adverse weather, 23–32.[8] The individual groups are admonished repeatedly by priestly guides to give thanks to the Lord: "Let these thank Yahweh for his love, *for his marvels on behalf of man"* (verses 8, 15, 21, and 31). Any rescue of a man from danger by God is praised here as a "marvel." Then, in verse 33, the psalm suddenly changes over to a praise of the divine greatness in nature:

Sometimes he turned rivers into desert,
springs of water into arid ground.
and
Or again, he turned a desert into sheets
of water,
and an arid country into flowing springs.
(35)

At the end of the psalm a sapiential saying follows in verse 43 as an exhortation not to overlook the love of Yahweh:

If you are wise, study these things
and realise how Yahweh shows his love.

Thus the love of God is manifested both in what he does for the salvation of mankind and in his deeds in nature. Consequently, questions like, Are there any miracles at all and are miracles not contrary or above nature? would have been unintelligible to early Israel. It is not until much later that such questions arise under the influence of Hellenism, as, for instance, the Book of Wisdom demonstrates.[9]

According to the Old Testament, miracles reveal God, his will, and his lordship. Frequently they are called " 'ôt," signs. Israel is to recognize her God by these signs; see particularly Exodus 10:1 f: "Then Yahweh said to Moses, 'Go to Pharaoh, for it is I who have made his heart and his courtiers stubborn, so that I could work these *signs* of mine among them; so that you can tell your sons and your grandsons how I made fools of the Egyptians and what *signs* I performed among them, to let you *know* that I am Yahweh.' "

Later, during the exile, Psalm 106 reproaches the "fathers": Verse 7

our ancestors in Egypt never grasped the meaning of your marvels.

They failed to appreciate your great love, they defied the Most High at the Sea of Reeds.

Verse 21

They forgot the God who had saved them

by performing such feats in Egypt,
such wonders in the land of Ham,
such fearful things at the Sea of Reeds.

Eighteen times we encounter the phrase "signs and wonders" in the Old Testament. This almost always occurs when there is some reference to the events surrounding the exodus. They are apparently rooted in the Deuteronomic perspective of history.[10] However, this means that the events surrounding the exodus of Israel from Egypt are later—in the *retrospective, prophetic interpretation of the early history of Israel* as related in the Pentateuch—interpreted throughout as "signs and wonders" of Yahweh which revealed the "strong hand" and the "outstretched arm" of Yahweh (see particularly Deuteronomy 26:8: "... and Yahweh brought us out of Egypt with mighty hand and outstretched arm, with great terror, and with *signs and wonders*. He brought us here and gave us this land, a land where milk and honey flow"). This kind of inspired interpretation of history has always a revelational and kerygmatic significance. When Deuteronomy was written, many centuries had passed since the events surrounding and preceding the settlement in the new land. Now Israel finally recognizes—this recognition is written down for all future generations—that her history was *divinely ordained* from the beginning.

In the light of this recognition many happenings accompanying the time of the exodus, of which the old traditions speak, are understood as "signs and wonders" of Yahweh, regardless of whether they have to do with a "wonderful" (in the original and strict sense of the word) or with a "merely profane" occurrence or not. In no way are we qualified to make concrete critical distinctions because we possess only the *accounts* of them in the Bible. These accounts, however, were written in the light of certain theological insights and certain kerygmatic purposes. Israel is to come to the realization that God has led her with his strong arm from the beginning, just as it was and is still the case in the creation and the sustenance of the world. Because God is the one who truly acts, his deeds throughout the history of Israel rightly deserve the name "signs and wonders," no matter whether these, his works, are expressly explained as such or not. Her history is a history miraculously guided by God: this Israel is to recognize![11] And this history guided by God is aiming at what is later called the $\beta\alpha\sigma\iota\lambda\epsilon\acute{\iota}\alpha$ $\tau o\tilde{\upsilon}$ $\theta\epsilon o\tilde{\upsilon}$, the universal kingship of God. *The miracles further the realization of this goal; the accounts of the miracles further the recognition of this goal.*

The wonders and signs of which the Old Testament speaks must, therefore, never be treated as isolated events. Moreover, the miracle is "integrated into the context of a history that is guided by God so that it never stands alone but always appears *as the serving link in a major whole.*"[12]

The synthesis of word and work which we encounter in the saving work of God according to the testimony of the Old Testament is equally found in the salutary acts of *Jesus the Messiah,* who, as the "Son of Man," is God's representative on earth. This is to be illustrated by several exam-

16

ples: the proclamation of Jesus about the close proximity of the kingdom of God (Mark 1:15)—that is, a revelation by word—finds immediate confirmation in the healing of a demoniac in the synagogue at Capernaum (Mark 1:23–28; verse 27: τί ἐστιν τοῦτο; διδαχὴ καινὴ κατ᾽ ἐξουσίαν!). The composition of the Sermon on the Mount (Matt 5–7) is followed by the magnificent cycle of miracles, with ten being recounted (Matt 8 f), concluding with the final remark: "Jesus made a tour through all the towns and villages, teaching in their synagogues, proclaiming the Good News of the kingdom and curing all kinds of diseases and sickness" (Matt 9:35). Sermons and healings are closely connected: both are manifestations of the kingdom of God which closes in already with Jesus. Particularly in the gospel which specifically emphasizes the word of Jesus in its revelational function, its "signs" are found in indissoluble unity: in the Gospel according to St. John (more about this below).

Now we are entering the second part of our discussion: the historical question. All the observations made above are a contribution to this very question. For it cannot be answered adequately unless the unity of word and work in the saving works of God and Jesus is recognized. A limitation of Jesus' revelational activity to the word is ultimately equal to unbiblical thinking. As far as the Bible is concerned, God is the one who acts through words and deeds.

But has Jesus of Nazareth worked any miracles at all? This question requires special attention because it is negatively answered by a rationalizing and "demythologizing" interpretation of the Bible.

THE TESTIMONY OF THE NEW TESTAMENT AND OF JUDAISM TO THE MIRACLE-WORKING OF JESUS

To begin with, it is undeniably certain that the four evangelists assert that Jesus of Nazareth worked miracles. Anyone taking Jesus for the one he is proclaimed to be by the gospels and the early Christian Church for the Redeemer who became flesh and the Son of God, does not doubt this assertion, at least not on principle.

18

The historical question in *this* sense is therefore above all a matter of a Christological decision on the part of faith. Anyone considering Jesus only as a rabbi or prophet who was inspired by a particular eschatological consciousness will readily voice his reservation against the contention that Jesus of Nazareth worked miracles. Yet, it is by no means necessary to revert immediately to our faith to "assure" the historicity of a miracle-working Jesus of Nazareth. An analysis of evangelical tradition itself offers assistance to arrive at a clear judgment.

I am proceeding from a saying of Jesus which belongs to the oldest tradition of the gospels, the logia of Jesus: from his lamentations over the Galilean towns of Chorazin, Bethsaida, and Capernaum (Matt 11:20–24; Luke 10:13–15). Matthew provided these lamentations of Jesus with an introduction in verse 20, which also offers an explanation for their cause: "Then he began to reproach the towns in which most of his miracles (δυνάμεις) had been worked, because they refused to repent." The first lamentation is directed against the town of Chorazin, situated about two miles north-west of Capernaum in a basaltic wilderness whose synagogue was excavated between 1905 and 1926.[13] The visitor is confronted with a huge field of ruins which unfortunately has not been examined to a great extent yet. According to Dalman it is quite likely that the city had an "active population" at the time of Jesus. Yet, according to the laments of Jesus over this city, it must have sadly lacked an understanding of the meaning of the miracles which he worked as the messenger of God in the cities of Galilee. The Chorazinians refused to repent in full view of his miracles just as did the people of Capernaum and Bethsaida, that is, they did not acknowledge Jesus as the Messiah of Israel; they remained unbelievers.[14]

Jesus' curse of these three cities of his native Galillee is very old according to a critical evaluation of tradition. "Old Aramaic tradition," says J. Jeremias.[15] As for the rest, we have knowledge only through this logion that Jesus also visited the city of

Chorazin and repeatedly performed miracles there (plural: αἱ δυνάμεις). Nowhere else does the evangelical tradition about Jesus mention Chorazin. This is worth noting. It is true that R. Bultmann remarks with respect to our logion: "In any case we have here a community formulation, since the sayings look back on Jesus' activity as something already completed, and presuppose the failure of the Christian preaching in Capernaum."[16] Of course the laments presuppose a "failure," not however of the Christian missionary sermon, but rather of the effectiveness of Jesus in his native Galilee. Historically speaking, the logion belongs to the period of the life of Jesus when the "Galilean spring" collapsed and Jesus finally entered on the road of sorrows. The omission of the name of the town of Chorazin in the remaining tradition of the gospels shows the lack of interest in this city on the part of the post-Easter Christian community.[17] If there is one pre-Easter logion, then it is the lament of Jesus over these three cities of his native Galilee! It belongs to the most authentic voice (*ipsissima vox*) of Jesus. If this is true, then the pre-Easter *ipsissima vox* of Jesus is itself proof enough for his miracle-working in Galilee. "Jesus is deeply moved by the imminent destruction which he envisions for the cities of Galilee. He is aware of their refusal to recognize in his miracles, in his healings and expulsions of evil spirits, the approaching kingdom of God. For all these signs are not able to make them repent."[18] Especially if one recognizes the indissoluble connection of the proclamation of Jesus about the already approaching kingdom of God with his "works of power"— where the unity of God's revelation by word and work, already noticeable in the Old Testament and mentioned above, is merely continued—one does not doubt that Jesus truly performed miracles. We will have to return to this interrelationship again in more detail (page 44 below).

The Beelzebul pericope,[19] too, which contains parts of a very old tradition, particularly in Luke,[20] clearly testifies to a miracle-working of Jesus, in partciular the saying of Jesus which was incorporated into

Mark's version by Matthew and Luke and
most likely stems from a logion of Jesus:
"And if it is through Beelzebul that I cast
out devils, through whom do your own
experts cast them out? Let them be your
judges, then. But if it is through the Spirit
of God that I cast devils out, then know
that the kingdom of God has overtaken
you" (Matt 12:27 f; Luke 11:19 f). The
dispute which we find in the Beelzebul
pericope shows us that the opponents of
Jesus do not dispute at all that he, like
their own "sons," is exorcising demons,
that is, his very adversaries are *witnesses
to his miracle-working* through their own
authentic witness of his exorcisms.[21] However, what they apparently dispute is the
authority with which he expels the evil
spirits.

The fact that we are confronted here
with a genuine bit of history from the pre-
Easter life of Jesus seems to be confirmed
by a Jewish tradition which is recorded
in the Babylonian Talmud (Sanhedrin
43[a]): "It was taught: On the eve of the
Passover, Yeshu was hanged. For forty days

before the execution took place, a herald[22] went forth and cried, 'He is going forth to be stoned because he has practiced sorcery and enticed Israel to apostasy. Anyone who can say anything in his favor, let him come forward and plead on his behalf!' But since nothing was brought forward in his favor, he was hanged on the eve of the Passover."[23]

The most interesting aspect about this talmudic passage in connection with our topic is the fact that Jewish tradition, too, gives evidence of Jesus' death and lists as reasons for his execution: "because he has practiced sorcery and enticed Israel to apostasy." This is a quite unequivocal reminiscence of the miracle-working of Jesus, just as it is recorded in the dispute of the Beelzebul pericope: Jesus of Nazareth "practiced magic" and thereby corrupted Israel because he cured demoniacs with the help of the devil.[24] The opponents of Jesus fail to recognize, just as the inhabitants of the cities of Galilee, that the miracles of Jesus, in particular the expulsion of demons, are an indication of the dawn of the kingdom of God. To them his acts are demonic acts of "witchcraft."

It stands to reason that the Christian community would be interested in passing on the dispute contained in the Beelzebul pericope, but less so because of an interest in the miracle-working of Jesus (per se) than because of the connection between the coming of the kingdom of God and the miracle-working of Jesus: *with him* the eschatological kingdom of God was and still is coming with all its forcefulness. The aforementioned talmudic note, however, lets us recognize that it was not first the *Christian* "interest" which made creative use of the Beelzebul tradition; rather, the expulsion of demons and the remaining miracles of Jesus were, indeed a decisive issue in the dispute between him and his adversaries in Israel.

Furthermore, it is striking that it is exactly the reference to the miracle-working of Jesus that has a central place in the missionary preaching of the early Church, as Acts 2:22 ("Jesus of Nazareth was a man commended to you by God by the *miracles* and *portants* and *signs* that God worked through him when he was among you, as you all know") and 10:38 ("God had anointed him with the Holy Spirit and with *power,* and because God was with him, Jesus went about *doing good and curing all who had fallen into the power of the devil").* Even though the formulation of these statements may stem from the pen of the author of the Acts of the Apostles,[25] their "structure, scriptural proof, and the number of archaisms in the speeches of Acts 1–13 nevertheless refer to an older tradition which was already part of the past at the time of Luke."[26] Particularly the reference to the miracle-working of Jesus seems to have belonged to the oldest topoi of missionary preaching.[27] This is all the more probable because in later Jewish tradition, too, "the miracle-working in the tradition about eschatological prophets, such as Moses, plays a decisive role," which "obviously assumed great significance primarily in view of Jesus' life on earth."[28]

These references must suffice, and indeed they are enough to dismiss any doubts about the historicity of Jesus' miracle-working. Yet it seems that the "historical proof" receives additional support through the following reflection: Can certain miracles of Jesus, in the form they are related in the gospels, be recognized as *ipsissima facta* of Jesus, that is, of deeds which are typical of him and which only he would have performed?

IPSISSIMA FACTA OF JESUS?

As is well-known, exegesis, in its extensive discussion of the "historical" Jesus, is searching for the *ipsissima vox* of Jesus, that is, for the word of Jesus as it is recorded *verbatim* in the tradition of the gospels. Exegesis has scored a certain amount of success in this respect.[29] However, is there also something like *ipsissima facta* in analogy to the *ipsissima vox* of Jesus?[30] The question must be answered in the affirmative, for there is not a shadow of a doubt that Jesus' ostentatious meals with the so-called publicans and sinners are such *ipsissima facta* (see for instance Mark 2:13–17: the dinner with the publican Levi). There also seems to exist a number of miracles of Jesus that must be considered as *ipsissima facta* of Jesus, namely, those which, like the meals of Jesus with the publicans, display a definite *anti-Pharisean front*. An example, namely, the account about the healing of a leper in Mark 1:40–45, may further illustrate this point:[31] "A leper came to him and pleaded on his knees: 'If you want to,' he said, 'you can cure me.' Feeling sorry for him, Jesus stretched out his hand and touched him [the Western text reads "he got angry"]. 'Of course I want to!' he said. 'Be cured!' And the leprosy left him at once and he was cured. Jesus immediately sent him away and sternly ordered him, 'Mind you say nothing to anyone, but go and show yourself to the priest, and make the offering for your healing prescribed by Moses as evidence of your recovery.' The man went away, but then started talking about it freely and telling the story everywhere, so that Jesus could no longer go openly into any town, but had to stay outside in places where nobody lived. Even so, people from all around would come to him."

The pericope strongly resists any smooth interpretation, especially in its version in Mark. Matthew and Luke obviously were already painfully aware of this, as their representation of the account evidences. It is primarily the peculiar behavior of Jesus that poses many a riddle, particularly if the version "he got angry" is to be taken as the original one—a fact for which the omission of this phrase in Matthew and Luke speaks. Why would Jesus get "angry"? Is it the anger of the Messiah at the power of death (see John 11:33–38: Jesus sighs with great "distress" as he approaches the tomb of Lazarus)? And is it not true that leprosy is called "Death's First-Born" in Job 18:13? Moreover, why does Jesus charge the cured man and send him immediately away? And why is it that Jesus can "no longer go openly into any town but has to stay outside in places where nobody lives" when people from all around would come to see Him? Verse 44 complicates the situation even more: Should it be translated as "evidence to them" or "evidence against them?"[32] "Evidence to them" would mean that Jesus acknowledged the legal regulations of the Old Testament about the treatment of lepers, although, simultaneously, he acts contrary to them by "touching" the leper. "Evidence against them," on the other hand, would probably mean: "If the actual cure is acknowledged by the priest, then this means a grave incrimination of the unbelief the people still adhere to."[33] Strathmann is apparently on the right track with his interpretation of εἰς μαρτύριον αὐτοῖς.

For what is the kerygmatic significance of Jesus' curing of the leper? To answer this question, we must proceed from the position of the leper within the religious community of Israel.[34] In Leviticus 13:45 f it says: "A man infected with leprosy must wear his clothing torn and his hair disordered; he must shield his upper lip and cry, 'Unclean, unclean.' As long as the disease lasts he must be unclean; and therefore he must live apart: he must live outside the camp." The leper is not "unclean" for hygienic reasons but from a cultic and

30

ritual point of view. Thus it reads in the Babylonian Talmud (Kelim 1:4): "He conveys uncleanness by entering into a house." And in the Siphra on Numbers (12, 12 §105 [28a]): "Just as a corpse in a tent [defiles all those with him in the same room], a leper, too, renders it unclean by entering it"; in 5, 2 §1 (1a): "All that the one stricken with discharge renders unclean is equally made unclean by the leper." In the Babylonian Talmud (Nega'im 13:11) it reads: "If a leper entered a house, all vessels in it, even to the height of the roof beams, become unclean"; and in Nega'im 13:7: "If an unclean man stood under a tree and a clean man passed by, the latter becomes unclean." According to Flavius Josephus (*Against Apion* I:31) lepers were forbidden either to stay in a city or to reside in a village, but had to be solitary vagrants; anyone who touches them is considered unclean. In his *The Jewish War* V:v,6 Josephus speaks of the exclusion of lepers from the "city," meaning Jerusalem. And in *The Jewish Antiquities* III:xi,3 it reads: "He [Moses]

banished from the city alike those whose
bodies were afflicted with leprosy . . . Lepers . . . he banished outright from the city,
to have intercourse with no man and as in
no way differing from a corpse." The
sacredness of the old walled cities in Pales-
tine consisted, according to Kelim 1:6 ff,
particularly in the fact that lepers were
excluded from them. See Numbers Rabbah VII:8 in Midrash Rabbah: "A walled
city is holier than the rest of the land, since
lepers may walk about in all the land but
may not do so in walled cities."

Leprosy was considered a punishment
for sins, especially for those who had sinned
with their tongues (slanderers and such).
Thus says Rabbi Jose ben Zimra (c. 220
A.D.): "He who slanders others will be
stricken by leprosy." Hubris, too, can cause
leprosy. The children of him who sleeps
with his wife during menstruation will become leprous. According to the Midrash
Rabbah (Leviticus Rabbah XVI:1) leprosy
is caused by haughty eyes, a lying tongue,
hands that shed innocent blood, a heart
that devises wicked thoughts, feet that are

swift to evil, a false witness that breathes out lies, and one that sows discord among brethren. Rabbi Jochanan (+279 A.D.) said: "All these are punished by leprosy."

Thus, leprosy was a terrible fate. A leper was considered a sinner, one punished by God. He was considered unclean and was therefore separated from the "clean." He was barred from the services in the Temple, for he was not permitted to enter the Holy City (he was permitted to participate in synagogue services in a special room only). He was treated like a dead man! "Four are accounted as dead: A poor man, a leper, a blind person, and one who is childless (Babylonian Talmud, Nedarim 64a).

One must know all this in order to understand the kerygma of our pericope. The pericope has been handed down without regard to either time or place. This, too, may be taken as a sign that the healing of the leper is nothing accidental but possesses programmatic significance within the messianic life of Jesus. The leper approaches Jesus, and Jesus does not avoid him, as it was customary among the rabbis for fear of contracting the disease and subsequently becoming unclean. Rabbi Johanan taught: It is prohibited to go four cubits to the east of a leper (Leviticus Rabbah XVI:3). Another rabbi even speaks of 100 cubits. Resh Lakish, who is responsible for this regulation, threw stones toward a leper when he came upon one, shouting: "Go to your place and do not defile other people." Rabbi Eleazar ben Simeon hid himself as soon as he caught sight of a leper. The rabbis Assi and Ammi would not enter a leper's alley. Rabbi Meir even went as far as refusing to eat an egg that came from an alley of lepers.[35]

Jesus acts quite differently. He touches the leper! He neither is afraid of a possible infection nor is the leper in his eyes an "unclean" person, contact with whom renders a man unclean. To Jesus the leper is obviously not a sinner chastised by God. By touching him he grants the sick man who had been excluded from the Temple services the proximity of God. For the supplication of the leper—"If you want to, you can cure me"—has a double meaning: he asks for health and for cleanness in order to be a full member of the community of Israel again. Not only does Jesus proclaim his cleanness as a priest would do, but he also cures the leper with his sovereign command: "I want you to be cured!"

Now we can also say why Jesus became "angry." He is not getting angry at the power of death, as it was conjectured; rather, he get angry at the injustice done to the lepers by Israel. This is the reason why Jesus stretches out his hand to the sick man, just as, according to the Bible, God stretches out his hand to take somebody under his protection. Thus Jesus takes the leper under the protection of God, and, by touching the sick man, he establishes a community together with him. All this happens in a rather demonstrative fashion. *The behavior of Jesus has a definite anti-rabbinical character!* This, too, is apparently the reason for the fact that Jesus sends the cured man immediately away and orders him sternly to show himself to the priest as "evidence against them." All

this is a manifestation of the holy anger of
Jesus at that false form of legalism with
which Israel proceeded against lepers and
at the pseudotheology which had developed in connection with it. By curing the
leper Jesus unmasks all this. That is why
his deed is "evidence against them,"
namely, against their self-righteousness
which had a wrong notion not only of the
leper but also of him together with whom
the eschatological kingdom of God, which
takes the sick, the poor, and the sinners under its protection, is overtaking Israel and
the world.

It is not until we have understood Jesus'
behavior as a front against the rabbis that
the historical question can be answered
correctly. We have seen that "analogies"
from the history of religion, which were
employed to bring some light into the account of the miraculous healing of the
leper, on principle cannot contribute
much. As long as one has not recognized
here the antirabbinical and anti-Pharisean
front of Jesus, one is speaking beyond the
actual kerygma in the interpretation of

the evangelical accounts of the cure of the leper. Yet, if one considers it as such, then one also recognizes an *ipsissimum factum* of Jesus. Such *ipsissima facta* of Jesus can be found in particular wherever it is impossible to draw an analogy from the history of religion, but where we encounter a single, unrepeatable situation of Jesus who, contrary to the "pious" beliefs of the leaders of His people, makes the true nature of the kingdom of God visible and thereby that of the Good News, not merely in words but also through his deeds. Bultmann, too, concedes: "The healing of the leper (Mark 1:40–45) will also have come from the Palestinian Church; σεαυτὸν δεῖξον τῷ ἱερεῖ κτλ. could hardly be formulated in an Hellenistic environment."[36] In fact, the entire pericope can be understood only on the basis of the historical situation of Jesus, and that means on the basis of *his* understanding of the kingdom of God.

There is a whole series of miracles of Jesus which possesses an antirabbinical and anti-Pharisean front, similar to the one of the curing of the leper according to Mark

37

1:40–45. It is mainly all the healings on the Sabbath that belong in this group. Moreover, in view of the rules of the Essenic community in 1 QSa II: 5 ff ("No one who is afflicted by any form of human uncleanness is to be admitted to the community, nor is anyone who becomes so afflicted to maintain his position within it. Similarly, no one who is afflicted with a bodily defect, who is stricken in hands or feet, who is lame or deaf or dumb, or who has any visible bodily defect, is to be admitted to a place among the 'dignitaries' for 'holy angels are in the congregation . . .' "[37]), many miracles of Jesus possess an additional anti-Essenian front: Jesus consciously heals those who were supposedly "punished" by God in order to demonstrate that it is exactly they who are members of the kingdom of God and of the community of the Messiah.[38] Having seen this, one recognizes these miracles as *ipsissima facta* of Jesus which are intimately linked up with and which cannot be separated from His historically proven arguments with the Scribes and Pharisees and their views.

Not only the word but also the accomplished facts, concretized in the form of miracles, reveal precisely Jesus' understanding of the kingdom of God and consequently the understanding of the gospels. Word and work form a synthesis in the life of Christ, as we already emphasized. The "anti-Pharisean" miracles of Jesus share certain aspects with analogies drawn from the history of religion only in as much as their stylistic principles and their phenomenal character are concerned, however not as regards their tendencies. We can therefore say that the historical question can neither be posed correctly nor be answered adequately unless we take the kerygmatic intentions in a miracle of Jesus into full account!

Yet, this has already led us right into the theological question about the significance and the function of the miracles of Jesus.

III

SIGNIFICANCE AND FUNCTION
OF THE MIRACLES OF JESUS

To ask for the "significance and function" of the miracles of Jesus means to try to determine how the miracles of Jesus are connected with his mission.

JESUS, THE MESSIANIC BEARER OF THE ESCHATOLOGICAL KINGDOM OF GOD

According to Mark 1:14 f, Jesus proclaims in his native Galilee the "Good News from God": "The time has come . . . and the kingdom of God is close at hand." The evangelist Mark sees in this logion of Jesus, which is technically speaking a typical call of a harbinger, a pronouncement of a program which is immediately executed by Jesus himself.[1] Thereby it is rather significant that, according to Mark, Jesus drives out a demon on the Sabbath immediately following the day of his proclamation: "In their synagogue just then there was a man possessed by an unclean spirit, and it shouted, 'What do you want with us, Jesus of Nazareth? *Have you come to destroy us?* I know who you are: the Holy One of God.' But Jesus said sharply, 'Be quiet! Come out of him!' And the unclean spirit threw the man into convulsions and with a loud cry went out of him. The people were so astonished that they started asking each other what it all meant. 'Here is a teaching that is new,' they said, 'and with authority behind it: he gives orders even to unclean spirits and they obey him.' And his reputation rapidly spread everywhere, through all the surrounding Galilean countryside" (Mark 1:23–28).

Why is it that, according to Mark, Jesus begins his ministry in Galilee with the expulsion of evil spirits? The reason for this must be seen in the "program" mentioned above. Jesus announced the *close proximity* of the kingdom of God (ἤγγικεν), because it is coming subsequent to the beginning of his ministry. And this dawn of the kingdom of God is visibly concretized in the powerful, irresistible "destruction" of the reign of Satan as manifested most particularly in the phenomenon of possession. That is why the "expulsion of evil spirits . . . belongs to Jesus' open war on the reign of Satan."[2] In the already mentioned logion from the Beelzebul pericope, "If it is through the Spirit of God that I cast devils out, then know that the kingdom of God has overtaken you," Jesus himself proclaims the indissoluble connection which exists between the arrival of the kingdom of God and *his* (ἐγώ) own ministry. Yet not only the expulsion of demons but also all the miracles of Jesus demonstrate—in any case, according to the synoptic tradition—the arrival of the eschatological kingdom of God at the instance of Jesus' appearance.[3] If we disregard this interrelationship between the miracles of Jesus and his message of the kingdom of God, we understand neither the miracles nor this message correctly. More about this below. At any rate, the significance and the function of the miracles of Jesus in connection with his ministry become clearly discernible only when we accept the conviction of the gospels that Jesus is the bearer of the eschatological kingdom of God. All three synoptics are agreed on this point, even though individual facets may differ.[4] The presently approaching and already arriving kingdom of God is in itself a "miracle"[5] in the eyes of Jesus, and it manifests itself as such particularly in his "works of power."

THE SALVATION OF THE KINGDOM OF GOD AND THE MIRACLES OF JESUS

Already from our previous discussion we gather that, according to the understanding of Jesus, the "kingdom of God" is not a "static affair," but rather something dynamic, a powerful *occurrence*. Jesus' behavior, in accordance with the kingdom of God and the announcement and the introduction thereof, is a powerful intervention in the affairs of the world.[6] When Jesus, according to Luke 10:9, sends out the seventy-two disciples and orders them, "Cure those in it [that is, in a city he has just come to] who are sick, and say 'The kingdom of God is very near to you!' " then the only meaning of this can be: "If a man is healed from his sickness by Jesus, then this means that God begins his reign through this very act of healing. Through such a healing the lordship of God is brought about,"[7] over Satan to be sure. For what is the outcome of the mission of the seventy-two? Luke relates it as follows: "The seventy-two came back rejoicing. 'Lord,' they said, 'even the devils submit to us when we use your name.' He said to them, *'I watched Satan fall like lightning from heaven*. Yes, I have given you power to tread underfoot serpents and scorpions and the *whole strength of the enemy;* nothing shall ever hurt you' " (Luke 10:17–19). The acting in accordance with and the message of the Good News of the kingdom of God as delivered by both Jesus and the

45

disciples powerfully overcome the reign of Satan, which is manifest everywhere in its terrible consequences.

A peculiar miracle of Jesus such as the cure of the Gerasene demoniac[8] reveals its kerygmatic significance as soon as one understands it as a powerful manifestation of God's lordship over Satan: the evil forces in the demoniac call themselves "legion" (Mark 5:9), that is, they consist of many demons (see verse 12). The demons beg Jesus for a new home in a herd of pigs that chanced to be feeding nearby—Mark gives their number at about two thousand, thereby consciously exaggerating, as the absence of a specific figure in Matthew and Luke clearly shows—but they only subsequently destroy that entire herd of pigs. "In the destruction of the herd of pigs the resistance of the demons against Jesus is continued . . . This clearly eliminates the frequently given interpretation . . . that all was merely a common farce about the cheated devils, this time attributed to Jesus. The structure of this narrative con-

tradicts such an interpretation, for in it
the struggle of the newly arrived kingdom
of God is described as it invades the realm
of Satanic power."⁹ It is only with this in
mind that we can rightly understand the
miracle of the cure of the Gerasene demoniac and the account thereof in the synoptic gospels as a powerful disarmament of
the false lord of the world, who vexes and
enslaves creation and whose victims can be
found even among the pigs. Through the
latter, a characteristic aspect of the reign
of Satan is revealed, that is, its *hatred
toward all creation,* which also expresses
itself, according to biblical belief, in catas-
trophes of nature, so that the "nature miracles" of Jesus, too, receive their special
meaning from this aspect. When he com-
mands the storm on the Sea of Galilee to
subside (see Mark 4:35–41; in Mark this
episode precedes the cure of the Gerasene
demoniac), he simultaneously tames the
demonic forces which manifest themselves
in the gale (see particularly Mark 4:39:
"And he woke up and rebuked the wind

47

and said to the sea, 'Quiet now! Be Calm!' And the wind dropped and all was calm again") .[10]

To Jesus, all the sick whom he heals and all the dead whom he raises are not people who were punished by God on account of their sins; rather, they are victims of the strong one rescued by one who is even stronger (see Mark 3:27). Thus, right from the beginning Jesus leads creation to salvation through his miracles, and it is exactly *through his miracles* that the salvation of the kingdom of God reveals itself.[11] This salvation embraces not only the "soul" of man but his body as well, and thus the whole of creation. Here, too, it is true: *caro cardo salutis* (the flesh is the hinge of salvation).[12] E. Käsemann rightfully remarks in view of the accounts of miracles in the gospels "that the New Testament most deeply incorporates miracles in its kerygma and that it does not restrict itself merely to forgiveness of sins, conversion, and faith as miracles by overrating the spiritual aspects. The New Testament is anxious to proclaim that God desires and addresses bodily existence eschatologically as well as in creation, that is, man in his totality in his world."[13]

The miracles of Jesus already delineate the reign of the Crucified of which particularly the epistles of St. Paul speak.[14] And when the salvation of the kingdom of God is evident in these miracles, then a miracle-working of Jesus in the sense testified by the gospels cannot be denied. Otherwise one does not comprehend the essence of Jesus' message of the kingdom of God which he had to deliver to Israel and the rest of the world. A limitation of Jesus' revelation activity to the word alone misses the essence of his mission and of his intentions—besides, it does not recognize the hope which is offered to the world through the miracles of Jesus (see chapter VI below).

THE MIRACLES OF JESUS AS CHRISTOLOGICAL REVELATION

"If the kerygma of Jesus had as its central objective the approaching *basileia* [kingdom] with its call to repent, then this certainly did already include a Christolog-ical self-revelation."[15] The same was al-ready said with regard to Jesus' program-matic opening logion in Galilee according to Mark 1:15 and particularly in connec-tion with the repeatedly mentioned logion from the Beelzebul pericope: "But if it is through the Spirit of God that I cast devils out, then know that the kingdom of God has overtaken you." Jesus' message of the *basileia* already contains a Christological self-revelation. This Christological impli-cation is consciously developed and ex-panded in the Gospel according to St. John, particularly because of the Johannine un-derstanding of the miracles of Jesus. Here the miracles of Jesus are called "signs" ($\sigma\eta\mu\epsilon\tilde{\iota}\alpha$), and "signs" they are of Christ and his salvation.[16]

We must mention here particularly the three great $\sigma\eta\mu\epsilon\tilde{\iota}\alpha$: the miracle of the loaves (John 6), the cure of the man born blind (John 9), and the resurrection of Lazarus (John 11). We will briefly look at the account about the cure of the man born blind (John 9) and how it relates to our topic because there a particularly clear presentation reveals the meaning pointedly. After the miracle was performed, the question of "how he had come to see" is discussed (John 9:10–15). This question led automatically to that of verse 17: "What have you to say *about him* yourself, now that he has opened your eyes?" At the instance of this question the cure of the man born blind presses for the fundamental Christological question, as the further conversations of the Pharisees and of Jesus himself with the cured man show (see John 9:12–38). The question is the "where from" of Jesus and his mystery (see John 9:29). First, the cured man identifies Jesus as a "prophet" (John 9:17). Asked by Jesus, "Do you believe in the Son of Man?" the cured man himself replies with a question. "Sir, tell me who he is so that I may believe in him." And Jesus replies: "You are looking at him; he is speaking to you." To this the cured man replied, "Lord, I believe" (John 9:35–38). With this Christological confession the Johannine account of the cure of the man born blind reaches its climax and objective. Essentially this means that the σημεῖα of Jesus which the fourth Gospel relates do operate as a Christological revelation which, to be sure, is inseparable from the soteriological function. They reveal Christ and his salvation.

Now the theological interpretation of the miracles of Jesus is strongly noticeable in the fourth Gospel in the sense just mentioned, having to do with the Johannine point of view,[17] but this theological interpretation merely explicates what already exists very clearly and perceptibly in the synoptic miracles of Jesus.[18] It was already the synoptic miracles which implied a Christology because they revealed the authority and power, the ἐξουσία of Jesus. Indeed, in the synoptic Gospels, too, there are accounts of miracles of Jesus which have a definite Christological function, for instance, the pericope about Jesus' walk on water (Mark 6:47–56; Matt 14:22–33), a true account of the *epiphany* (manifestation) of Jesus.

We have sufficiently seen now the significance and the function of the miracles of

Jesus and, at the same time, we also realize that the historical question of the miracles of Jesus can neither be asked correctly nor can it be answered thus unless their significance and function are taken into consideration. It is very easy to talk past the subject, then, and the historical question never really becomes tangible. However, the historical quest for the miracles of Jesus has yet another side at which we have already hinted somewhat when we were briefly touching the theological interpretation of the miracles of Jesus in the Gospel according to St. John. I am speaking of their form-critical side which will be discussed in the following chapter, though we will have to restrict our investigation to the most essential points.

IV

THE FORM-CRITICAL QUESTION: THE MIRACLES OF JESUS IN THE TRADITION OF THE GOSPELS

Why are we to face this question at all? Because we must make a basic distinction between a miracle on the one hand and the account thereof on the other. The miracle is the event; the account, the narrative about it. They are not identical as everybody knows. A narrative, an account, contains a fundamentally subjective element, specifically, the mind of the narrator. No matter how hard a narrator, speaking from personal experience, may trouble himself to eliminate any form of "prejudgment" and to submit a "neutral" report, already the first impression of and the "exposure" to an event employs value judgments and subjective interpretation, no matter how unpretentious or primitive. M. Heidegger told us about this in *Being and Time*. The perspective of the observer is determined already by "prejudgments" from a linguistic point of view, because any form of speech represents in itself a certain interpretation of the world.

Thus, the "primitive accounts" of the miracles of Jesus were already characterized by "prejudgments," and we can immediately determine their nature: they were mainly Christological in nature. The very moment somebody follows Christ as a believer, his perspective becomes drastically changed (even *before Easter,* which is sometimes overlooked!). Indeed, from this moment on he views the words and deeds of Jesus like one who has taken sides with him. That is why it is possible for Christ finally to tell the cured man born blind that the blind will see and those with sight turn blind (John 9:39). He means that in a spiritual sense. The man born blind did not merely become one who sees physically, but he was turned into a man who

can see from within, too, because he came
to believe in Jesus. The Pharisees, on the
other hand, who claim to have sight turn
blind as Jesus charges (John 9:40 f). What
is true of the cured man born blind is
equally true of the disciple on a larger
scale: he sees Jesus in a light different from
those not involved and even more so from
the adversaries of Jesus, no matter how far
his way to actual belief may yet be.

We are immediately approaching the
form-critical question which arises necessarily in conjunction with the miracles of
Jesus. For what we encounter in the gospels are *accounts* of the miracles of Jesus,
and, consequently, what has just been said
applies to the reporters of the gospels as
well: they are conditioned by their prejudices. To proceed right to the core of the
question, is it possible that the primitive
accounts of miracles of Jesus are already
characterized by the prejudices of the post-
Easter, the Christological, perspective of
faith which is already an *interpretation* in
itself? If we answer affirmatively, is it possible, then, that the "actual" historical

occurrence can still be made out?

Questions like these are rather difficult to answer. Yet, we might give it a try with a particularly difficult example which has already been mentioned above, that is, Jesus' walk on the Sea of Galilee which all three evangelists report[1] and which is one of "the most interesting passages in the gospels from the point of view of the history of tradition."[2] The fact that the fourth Gospel, too, mentions it has to do with the distinct "epiphanic character" of this miracle of Jesus. But what historical facts are hidden beneath this epiphanic narrative? Can they still be reconstructed? Or does this narrative merely serve the subsequent "illustrations" of the homologesis of the early Church which confesses Jesus Christ as the Son of God? Mark's version of the pericope seems to resist such an interpretation. It concludes on a completely negative note: "They were utterly and completely dumbfounded because they had not (yet) seen what the miracle of the loaves meant; their minds were closed" (Mark 6:51–52; special version!). Compared with the conclusion of the same pericope in Matthew, it sounds entirely different: "The men in the boat bowed down before him and said, 'Truly you are the Son of God'" (Matt 14:33). In John, finally, we encounter the typical *concentration christologique*. Here the pericope climaxes in the epiphanic formula "It is I" (John 6:20).

One might object that in the conclusion of Mark, too, a typically Marcian motif becomes noticeable, that is, that of the stupidity of the disciples.[3] The question remains whether this motif still makes sense from the point of view of a post-Easter reflection on the mystery of Jesus. This question suggests itself all the more urgently, since already Matthew did obviously not appreciate this motif and concludes the pericope, therefore, with a clear profession of the disciples that Jesus is the Son of God. To be sure, it is tremendously difficult to reconstruct precisely what the actual historical occurrence was like when Jesus walked on the sea. Already Mark's narrative reveals a definite preoccupation with the revelational content of the event, as he shows in the ἐγώ εἰμι— (I am-) formula of Jesus.[4] This gives rise to great inconsistencies already in Mark, not to speak of improbabilities as far as the course of events is concerned. E. Haenchen compiled all these in his commentary to the Gospel of Mark, not without a certain irony.[5] But since Mark pursues his "tendency" by means of this narrative, he fails to offer a realistic presentation of the facts. "All the questions raised by us did not concern the narrator."[5] Perhaps he was not even aware of them. "His mind is fixed on Jesus and his activities."[5]

We must nevertheless guard ourselves against a conclusion that boils down to a denial of any historicity to the event on account of the unrealistic character of the narrative, as, for instance, Haenchen does.[6] Yet Haenchen himself makes a remark which might help us along: "The reality of the disciples before Easter and the belief of the post-Easter community to which the risen Christ appeared cannot be united without breaking up the continuity of the passage."[7] They can be united subsequently without the danger of losing continuity as Matthew's pericope proves: the epiphany of Jesus on the Sea of Galilee corresponds adequately to the profession of the Son of God! The tension, however, of which Mark reports, between the powerful epiphany of Jesus on the Sea of Galilee and the peculiar behavior of the disciples, still reflects clearly the kind of a position the disciples were in vis-à-vis Jesus of Nazareth before Easter: *he is to them an as yet unsolved riddle.* They are certainly moved by the divine mystery, yet Jesus' true nature is still concealed to them and generally incomprehensible. The very dialectic of the "messianic mystery" *belongs to the pre-Easter Jesus,* not the post-Easter one, that is, the dialectical relationship and tension between revelation and concealment.[8]

Jesus' walking on the Sea of Galilee is the revelation of an authority which belongs to God only according to the belief of the Old Testament (see Job 9:8: "He and no other stretched out the skies, and trampled the Sea's tall waves"), one which,

61

however, is immediately going into hiding behind the anonymity of the carpenter from Nazareth. What happened historically during that night on the Sea of Galilee seems to have been the following: Jesus came miraculously to the aid of his disciples when they were in distress, and he declared himself with the ambiguous formula "It is I." Yet, initially the recognition of the disciples touched only slightly on the mystery of his person without grasping its essence, a fact which Mark expresses as follows in his conclusion: "They were utterly and completely dumbfounded because they had not seen what the miracle of the loaves meant; their minds were closed." They merely experienced the *tremendum* of the holy, but not yet the *mysterium*.

Matthew shortens the pericope and de-emphasizes the fear of the disciples by letting them confess unanimously the divine sonship of Jesus: "The men in the boat bowed down before him and said, 'Truly, you are the Son of God.' " But before they say this, Matthew inserts an addition of his own by letting also Peter walk on the sea; this is an interpolation which carries the typical linguistic characteristics of Matthew. Matthew must have come upon this addition someplace else. He worked it over and inserted it into the pericope, because the location (that is, Jesus' walking on the sea) seemed to him perfectly fit for this purpose. To be sure, this takes away from the pericope the conciseness it has in Mark, but Matthew gains, instead, an excellent opportunity to refute faintheartedness in face of the divine mystery of Jesus, which he subsequently enhances by having the disciples confess the divine sonship of Jesus, and he thereby presents a mirror image of the faith of the post-Easter Church. Yet, this post-Easter confession of faith which Matthew has the disciples make vicariously for the Church is perfectly in line with the events surrounding Jesus' walk on the sea and the as-yet-enigmatic "signs." The confession explicates the kerygmatic "declarative content" of the epiphanic event which occurred while Jesus was walking on the sea.

In John everything is directed toward this epiphanic event which itself reaches its climax in the strictly Christologically understood revelational formula ἐγώ εἰμι (It is I). That entire fear of the disciples which Mark reports is reduced to the fear motif which anyway is a necessary by-product of the epiphanic report (see John 6:19). After the revelation of Jesus everything is clarified; there are no further problems, neither for the disciples nor for Peter: "They were for taking him into the boat, but in no time it reached the shore at the place they were making for" (John 6:21). From a chronological point of view this means that the Christological faith of the early Church is now fully developed, and this full development is reflected in the Johannine presentation of the pericope.[9]

The passage dealing with Jesus' walk on the Sea of Galilee is, therefore, a perfect example for the form-critical problem in connection with the accounts of miracles in the gospels.[10] The differing representations of the tradition become visible in their respective purposiveness, and the influence of homologesis on the formation of a tradition becomes evident. Thus it becomes equally clear how necessary it is to distinguish between the miracle itself and the accounts thereof.[11] There are no "neutral" accounts of the miracles of Jesus in the New Testament.

Yet, a miracle does not happen at just any time and in full view of everybody. It depends on faith and evokes faith in turn. This shall be our next point.

V

FAITH AND THE MIRACLES
OF JESUS

At the end of the Nazareth pericope we read in Mark: "And he could work no miracle there, though he cured a few sick people by laying his hands on them. He was amazed at their lack of faith" (Mark 6:5 f). Here we encounter an obvious connection between the miracle-working of Jesus and the unbelief of his fellow countrymen: Jesus *"could (ἐδύνατο) not"* work any miracles in Nazareth because he did not find any faith there. "To be sure, this does not mean that it is faith itself that has the power to bring about miracles,"[1] but in order for a miracle to happen there must be faith on the part of those who beg

Jesus for help. The father of the demonic boy says to Jesus: "If you can do anything, have pity on us and help us. 'If you can?' retorted Jesus. 'Everything is possible for anyone who has faith.' Immediately the father of the boy cried out, 'I do have faith. Help the little faith I have!' " (Mark 9:22–24). "Through this paradox of belief and unbelief faith becomes genuine and capable of receiving the miracle of God, as the story wants to point out."[1] Faith, even though it may be weak and unrefined, is an absolute must if Jesus is to work a miracle. That is why Jesus says repeatedly to the cured men and women: "Your faith has saved you" (Matt 9:22; Mark 10:52; Luke 17:19).

The adversaries of Jesus, too, witness his "works of power," yet it does not change them from unbelievers into believers. They interpret these deeds as sorcery as the Beelzebul pericope shows—and as we already heard, Jesus was hanged, according to an old talmudic tradition, because he practiced magic. Rather, his adversaries demand of him "a sign from heaven" (Luke 11:16; Mark 8:11). But when the crowds became bigger, he began to speak: "This is a wicked generation; it is asking for a sign. The only sign it will be given is the sign of Jonah" (Luke 11:29), that is, none other than the parousia.[2] Jesus refuses to work spectacular miracles and to be viewed as a "wonder-worker." He retreats from the crowds with the realization that they believe in his name only when they see the signs that he gives (John 2:23 f). The first thing he says to the royal official is: "You will not believe unless you see signs and portents!" (John 4:48). To be sure, the crowds admire his "works of power," but they do not come to believe in him who works them. They do not recognize the miracles as "signs" which are to reveal Jesus as the divine Redeemer. They remain stuck in earthly things: ". . . you are not looking for me because you have seen the signs but because you had all the bread you wanted to eat" (John 6:26).

Contrary to them, the disciples recognize the "sign" as the manifestation of the "glory" of the Messiah, and they believe in him (John 2:11). The fatal sickness of Lazarus is destined for "God's glory, and through it the Son of God will be glorified" (John 11:4), and when Jesus woke Lazarus from the dead, many "believed in him" because they "had seen what he did" (John 11:45). The chief priests and the Pharisees, on the other hand, call a meeting in the Sanhedrin and say: "Here is this man working all these signs and what action are we taking?" (John 11:47); and they decide to have Jesus killed (John 11:53), not only him but Lazarus as well, "since it was on his account that many of the Jews were leaving them and believing in Jesus" (John 12:11).

The Johannine Christ then says rightfully at the conclusion of the pericope of the cure of the man born blind: "It is for judgement that I have come into this world, so that those without sight may see and those with sight turn blind" (John 9:39), and the Gospel continues: "Hearing this, some Pharisees who were present said to him, 'We are not blind, surely?' Jesus replied: 'Blind?' If you were you would not be guilty, but since you say, "We see," your guilt remains' " (John 9:40 f).

Thus we see that the relationship between miracle and faith cannot be expressed by a smooth formula. On the one hand, the miracles of Jesus are intended to evoke and not to force faith. They can never force faith because, on the other hand, they already presuppose this very faith, however not just any faith, but the belief that with Jesus the eschatological kingdom of God has overtaken the world and that Jesus reveals himself in his miracles as the One whom the Christian community subsequently confesses and proclaims. The miracles of Jesus possess, as it was rightly claimed, the *character of a call and decision*.[3] And this remains valid to our present day.[4]

VI

THE MIRACLES OF JESUS
AND THE HOPE OF
THE WORLD

Because the miracles of Jesus are insep-
arably connected with his proclamation
and his understanding of the eschatological
kingdom of God and its salvation (see
pages 41f above), and because the kingdom
of God represents the future of the world,
the hope of the world manifests itself in
the miracles of Jesus. Indeed, the miracles
contain a *promise*, that is, the promise that
the world will be led by God to salvation
in the manner already indicated and ini-
tiated by the miracles of Jesus. That is
why the miracles of Jesus are *signa prog-
nostica*, signs pointing into the future. Like
the kingdom of God, they, too, are escha-

tological in character. They are signs "which concern man's own fervently sought future salvation and for the general mediation of which the subjectively experienced testimonial (in contrast to a "reportage") is not accidental but essential."[1] The miracles of Jesus address man in his desire "to find meaning and salvation in his existence, an attitude which manifests itself in all the pronounced or latent, accepted or rejected, plans for his future, thereby giving his destiny a historical perspective.

Accordingly, a miracle is by no means an arbitrary demonstration on the part of God. It rather stands in a context of universal promise and fulfillment: as a convincing anticipation of the eschatological healing and saving power of God which has finally overtaken mankind for all time with the coming and resurrection of Jesus Christ."[2] The world yearns for salvation. All that historical scheming has ever been put forth in the history of mankind speaks eloquently of this fact, as, for instance, the Marxist phenomenon illustrates. Also the

sick and the possessed, whom Jesus cured,
grappled for salvation, and Jesus gave them
a foretaste of salvation by restoring them
to health. Thereby he announced distinctly
the coming salvation of creation. In the
eyes of Jesus man is sick in soul and body
as well, and Jesus want to heal him. "In the
gospels sickness appears as a decisive factor
in the characterization of man. From the
very beginning of the appearance of the
Son of Man until the end of his ministry
people appear before him with every con-
ceivable sickness. From fever to blindness,
from paralysis to leprosy . . . sickness is part
of man's destiny before the advent of the
Son of Man."[3] That is why Jesus works, not
just any miracle, but only those which are
connected with this task of healing the
world and, in it, man.

The kingdom of God which Jesus ush-
ers in is not an imaginary "superstructure"
which would not have anything to do with
concrete creation. The kingdom of God is
related to creation *as is,* and its desire is
to lead it to salvation. For that reason, the
hope of the world becomes manifest in the

miracles worked by Jesus of Nazareth. To deny the miracles of Jesus is, therefore, the same as to "drift away from the hope promised by the Good News" (Col 1:23). No matter how hard that world tries, and despite outward success, it will never reach ultimate salvation all by itself, as the historical experience of the human race so poignantly teaches. "It was not for any fault on the part of creation that it was made unable to attain its purpose, it was made so by God; but creation *still retains the hope* of being freed, like us, from its slavery to decadence, to enjoy the same freedom and glory as the children of God. From the beginning *until* now the entire creation, as we know, has been groaning in one great act of giving birth" (Rom 8:20–22). The failure "to attain its purpose" and the "decadence" which creation is subject to for the time being become apparent at any hour of history in sickness and in death and in the domination by the "powers and forces" which threaten creation.[4] Yet, according to the Apostle, creation can still cling to the hope that it will reach ultimate salvation in God. This hope already revealed itself to the world in the miracles of Jesus so that man may experience an anticipation of salvation to come. Such a hope includes freedom. When Jesus heals the sick and the possessed and when he wakes the dead, he then leads them to freedom, because he frees them of the "slavery of decadence." "As the prospect of salvation, of life, and of freedom, hope is a prospect of glory as well. . . . The glory which awaits us in Christ in such a way that it brightens our life despite its future character is a powerful reflection of the freedom of life eternal within the realm of salvation. . . ."[5]

If it is particularly in the *miracles* of Jesus that the hope of the world becomes manifest, then this means also that it is ultimately God alone who can free the world and help it in its affliction and in its addiction to the vainglorious and corruptive forces of death. Thus, the miracles of Jesus are an *act of that love* which God shows for the world in order to redeem it. For that reason the miracles of which the Bible,

and particularly the gospels, speak belong
to the story of salvation, which, to be sure,
is acted out in the history of mankind, yet
which is never identical with it because salvation, as an absolutely transcendental
mystery, is solely at the disposition of God
and never at man's.[6] This "negative dis-
posability" of a salvation which results
from the freedom of God is particularly
emphasized by the fact that the future salvation of the world is anticipated in miracles which are above and beyond man.
Thus, the miracles which the Bible relates
stress the fundamental principle of love
which becomes effective in every divine act
of salvation. But the salvation that revealed
itself through Jesus Christ is directed toward the concrete world, and that is why
the difference between the history of salvation and profane history is embraced by
Christ himself.

Thus, hope is given to the world that it
will be freed "from its slavery to decadence, to enjoy the same freedom and glory
as the children of God." This hope is most

"tangible" in the miracles of Jesus which "illustrate" the salvation brought about by the kingdom of God. For that very reason it is impossible that the "original foundation of a possible experience of miracles . . . is the method we use in observing phenomena in nature; for the scientific method proceeds from the methodical presumption that everything in the world is basically predictable and controllable. The sciences operate on the basis of a kind of "methodological determinism." It is not until then that a purely observational attitude becomes possible, because it is this "methodological determinism" that lets us perceive reality in any given case on account of the scientific data observed. . . . Because of these and other reasons . . . it is advisable to determine miracles not negatively as an "intervention" or in "violation" of natural causes, but positively as signs of the incorporation of total reality into the historical economy of God. . . ."[7] The eschatological kingdom of God is this very "economy of God." The miracles of Jesus are an essential part thereof, and, for that reason, the hope of the world becomes manifest in them.

VII

THE MIRACLES OF JESUS AND THE "DEMYTHOLOGIZATION OF THE NEW TESTAMENT"

The so-called demythologization of the New Testament is chiefly directed against Christology. For the intention to demythologize presupposes that Jesus was made only posthumously into what the post-Easter faith professes him to be—the Christ, the Son of God. This is supposed to have happened by "transferring" "concepts" of Judaism or pagan Hellenism to Jesus. The fact, too, that miracles were attributed to Jesus in the tradition of the gospels is supposed to be related to this transfer process, the purpose of which is said to have been to emphasize in a mythological fashion the "significance" ("meaning") of Jesus for faith.

If we consider the term "significance" a little more deeply in connection with R. Bultmann's program to demythologize the New Testament, then the question of *why* Jesus became "significant" to the disciples and the Church readily sugests itself. Bultmann would probably reply: Because the disciples felt Jesus' eschatological "call for decision" in their religious existence. Only now, through Jesus, do they recognize who God is and what they are before God. Through Jesus they arrive at a true understanding of God and self. But why exactly through *Jesus*? The New Testament supplies the answer: Because the disciples recognized in Jesus the Christ and the Son of God, to be sure, not overnight but after a long process which was only brought to a conclusion with the appearances of the risen Christ after Easter and the descent of the Holy Spirit at Pentecost.

The "significance" of Christ cannot simply be the result of, rather it must have been already the cause for, the "Christologization" of Jesus. This cannot be explained here extensively and in great detail because it would go beyond the framework of our topic. It is enough to say: "The eschatological call of Jesus for decision" cannot have been the sole reason for his Christologization. Whoever thinks he could assume this would find his views readily contradicted by analogous phenomena from the history of religion: Mohammed had perhaps an even more distinct eschatological consciousness than Jesus.[1] Nevertheless, he was not made into something like a Christ, let alone into the Son of God! On the contrary, Mohammed remained nothing else but the prophet who preached God as the one who is radically "different," and who promulgated God's absolute transcendence, although miracles were attributed to Mohammed, too. Jesus of Nazareth, on the other hand, was proclaimed the Christ and the Son of God soon after his death.

There must have been a different reason aside from the eschatological call of Jesus for decision. The reason must have resided *within him* himself, within his nature. It manifested itself in his unique awareness of his messianic mission, even though he never categorically referred to himself with names as "Messiah" or "Son of God." Jesus' awareness of his messianic mission and his self-confidence, indeed, revealed themselves, not in specific terms (aside perhaps from the ambiguous and enigmatic term "Son of Man"), but through his concrete words and deeds. What can be gathered about Jesus' self-confidence from the oldest tradition about the Jesus of the gospels when a definite "confession" was still absent is the following: *Jesus understood his ministry in Israel generally as an announcement of salvation.*[2] This ministry, however, implied a Christology which later was to find adequate/inadequate linguistic expression in the name "Christ." This identification is also intimately connected with the fact that particularly the gospels understand the miracles of Jesus as ἔργα τοῦ Χριστοῦ, as "works *of the Christ*" (see Matt 11:2). This means that it is exactly in the miracles of Jesus that his quality as "the Christ" is revealed; certainly not in them alone, but in them in a special way.

For the "works of the Christ" are decisively connected with the "announcement of salvation" of Jesus, the main content of which is the arrival of the eschatological kingdom of God.

For that reason it can be said that without the miracles which the gospels attribute to Jesus he is not the Christ, the Savior of Israel and the nations of the world. Through his miracles the coming of the kingdom of God is *articulated* with all the various aspects which belong to the total salvation of the world. These are lost as soon as a demythologization in the interpretation reduces the purpose of the miracles of Jesus existentially to their "significance." For the latter it does, indeed, not matter what kind of miracles Jesus worked. For such an interpretation the announcement of Jesus' rise from the dead would be enough. Through this the problematic and ambiguous character of the term "significance" ("meaning") becomes obvious: What "actually" constitutes that significance of Jesus which is to be emphasized by mythologizing the accounts of miracles?

The answer to this question must necessarily remain nebulous and uncommitting.

In a myth the truth shines forth,[3] even in the ancient tales about miraculous "divine men." Through them the truth that the world is in dire need of salavation becomes evident. If Jesus of Nazareth worked miracles and if, thereby, that hope shows forth which was given to the world by God, then he also confirms, simultaneously, the truth of that myth through which salvation and damnation of the world are preferably articulated. St. Augustine gave credit to the original truth that is hidden beneath a myth: "The thing itself which now is formally called the Christian religion already existed among the ancients. It has existed ever since the beginning of the human race until Christ became flesh. From that time on, the true religion which has always existed began to be called the Christian one."[4] A merely "existential" interpretation of the miracles of Jesus and their accounts in the gospels in the name of "demythologization" misses that very point that has been made in the latter from the very beginning. It strips Jesus of the quality of being the Christ—that is, the bearer of salvation—to all the nations of the world. Without the miracles of Jesus there is no Christ.

VIII

CONCLUSION

Much was said about the miracles of Jesus, even though we were unable to discuss everything that could and would have had to be said about them. The basic ideas presented here would still have to prove their correctness in an individual interpretation of the accounts of the miracles in the gospels. Still, we were able to contribute a few points to the discussion of the topic "The Miracles of Jesus." Hopefully this will help us along toward a more comprehensive understanding.

Thus it became clear that the historical question was not insoluble with respect to the miracles of Jesus. We saw that they cannot be solved adequately unless we take into account the theological and form-critical questions which suggest themselves in the evangelical accounts of the miracles of Jesus. It became fundamentally clear that only a perspective which takes the totality of the *story of salvation* into consideration can truly recognize the importance and meaning of the miracles of Jesus. To see the effect of the helping and healing hand of God in history, however, ultimately presupposes faith. Without this faith there is still no access to the miracles of Jesus even today.

NOTES

I THE PROBLEM

1. The literature concerning the question of miracles in the Bible is immense. Part of it was compiled by H. Haag, J. Schmid, and A. Vögtle, *LThK* ²X (Freiburg, 1957–1967) 1254 f, 1261; see J. Gnilka, *Handbuch Theologischer Grundbegriffe* II (Munich, 1963) 885; H. van der Loos, *The Miracles of Jesus* (Leiden, 1965) 705–726, presently the most important work on our topic; see F. Mussner, *BZ* 11 (1967) 139–141; Br. M. Metzger, *Index to Periodical Literature on Christ and the Gospels* (Leiden, 1966) 18–21; A. Vögtle, "Jesu Wunder einst und heute," *Bibel und Leben* 2 (1961) 234–254; G. Schille, *Die urchristliche Wundertradition. Ein Beitrag zur Frage nach dem irdischen Jesus* (Berlin, 1966).

II THE HISTORICAL QUESTION

1. See L. Köhler, *Lexikon in Veteris Testamenti Libros* (Leiden, 1953) 201; also the important remarks in J. Barr, *Bibelexegese und moderne Semantik* (Munich, 1965) 133–143.

2. See for more detail H. Lubsczik, "Wort-schöpfung und Tatschöpfung. Zur Entwicklung der priesterlichen Schöpfungslehre in Gen 1:1–2,4," *Bibel und Leben* 6 (1965) 191–208.

3. *Ibid.* 204.

4. See the interpretation of this psalm in H.-J. Kraus, *Psalmen II* (Neukirchen, 1961) 951.

5. *Ibid.* 950.

6. See also Th. Blatter, *Macht und Herrschaft Gottes* ("Studia Friburgensia NF," 29 [Fribourg, 1962]), a work which deserves special attention.

7. H. Haag, *LThK* [2]X, 1253; see also G. Quell, "Das Phänomen des Wunders im Alten Testament," *Festschrift für W. Rudolph* (Tübingen, 1961) 253–300.

8. See F. Nötscher, "Die Psalmen," *Echter Bibel,* Ps 107.

9. For more detail see G. Ziener, "Die theologische Begriffssprache im Buche der Weisheit," *BBB* 11 (Bonn, 1956) 148–158.

10. See K. H. Rengstorf, *ThW* VII, 214.

11. See also J. Schreiner, "Führung—Thema der Heilsgeschichte im Alten Testament," *BZ* 5 (1961) 2–18.

12. W. Eichrodt, *Theologie des Alten Testaments* II (Leipzig, 1935) 85.

13. For more information on Chorazin see G. Dalman, *Orte und Wege Jesu* (Gütersloh,

1924) 163–165; C. Kopp, *Die heiligen Stätten der Evangelien* (Regensburg, 1959) 243–246

14. "From this moment on, conversion means to join the messianic movement and the community in Jesus, because of the miracles which Jesus . . . worked in Chorazin and Capernaum. . . . In view of this evident reign of God (manifested in the powerful signs of Jesus) Jesus' contemporaries should have decided for Him" (E. Neuhäusler, *Anspruch und Antwort Gottes. Zur Lehre von den Weisungen innerhalb der synoptischen Jesusverkündigung* [Düsseldorf, 1962] 130 f).

15. J. Jeremias, *Jesu Verheißung für die Völker* (Stuttgart, 1956) 42 (fn 169). The body of the logion is handed down almost verbatim by the two independently working evangelists Matthew and Luke (see Matt 11:21–23 with Luke 10:13–15); this, too, is to be taken as an indication of a very old tradition. The logion received its final form at a very early date. It belongs to the pre-Easter logion tradition (see further below).

16. R. Bultmann, *The History of the Synoptic Tradition,* translated by John Marsh (New York, 1963) 112.

17. See E. Neuhäusler, *Anspruch und Antwort Gottes* (Düsseldorf, 1962) 200 f. W. Grundmann, too, remarks about the lamentations of Jesus over the cities of Galilee: "They

may very well date back to Jesus himself, since the tradition is not decisively determined by them" (*Das Evangelium nach Lukas* [Berlin, n.d.] 211).

18. Neuhäusler, *op. cit.* 202.

19. See Matt 12:35–37; Mark 3:23–30; Luke 11:17–23.

20. See for instance the analysis in W. Grundmann, *Das Evangelium nach Lukas* (Berlin, n.d.) 236 f.

21. See Grundmann on Luke 11:20.

22. See Sanhedrin VI. 1, The Babylonian Talmud: When somebody is led out to be stoned, a herald precedes him, crying: "So and so, the son of so and so, is going forth to be stoned because he committed such and such an offense . . . whoever knows anything in his favor, let him come and state it."

23. According to H. L. Strack, *Jesus, die Häretiker und die Christen nach den ältesten jüdischen Angaben* (Leipzig, 1910) 18*. See also J. Klausner, *Jesus von Nazareth* (Jerusalem, 1952) 29–31.

24. Justinus, too, remarks (*Dialogue with Trypho, A Jew*, 69, 7): "But though they (the Jews) saw such works, they asserted it was magical art. For they dared to call Him a *magician. . . .*"

25. See U. Wilckens, *Die Missionsreden in der Apostelgeschichte* (Neukirchen, 1961) 122 f, 46–50.

26. B. M. F. van Iersel, *"Der Sohn Gottes" in den synoptischen Jesusworten* (Leiden, 1964) 50, particularly 31–51.

27. E. Käsemann even sees old confession formulae incorporated in Acts 2:22 and 10:38 (*RGG* 3 VI, 1835).

28. F. Hahn, *Christologische Hoheitstitel. Ihre Geschichte im frühen Christentum* (Göttingen, 1963) 388.

29. See above all J. Jeremias, "Kennzeichen der ipsissima vox Jesu," *Abba, Studien zur neutestamentlichen Theologie und Zeitgeschichte* (Göttingen, 1966) 145–152.

30. I am indebted for this term to a talk given by J. B. Bauer (Graz).

31. Essentially I am repeating here what I wrote in *Katechetische Blätter* 91 (1966) 100–104.

32. Translators footnote: The version of *The Jerusalem Bible* (Garden City, 1966) avoids the problem altogether: ". . . go and show yourself to the priest, and make the offering for your healing prescribed by Moses as evidence of your recovery" (Mark 1:44).

33. H. Strathmann, *ThW* IV, 488 f.

34. See particularly H. L. Strack and P. Billerbeck, *Kommentar zum Neuen Testament aus Talmud und Midrasch* IV (Munich, 1928) 745–763.

35. According to W. Grundmann, *Das Evangelium nach Markus* (Berlin, n.d.) 53.

36. R. Bultmann, *The History of the Synoptic Tradition,* 240.

37. Translators footnote: "Manual of Discipline for the Future Congregation of Israel," *The Dead Sea Scriptures in English Translation,* with introduction and notes by Theodore H. Gaster (Garden City, 1964) 329.

38. See also G. Delling, "Botschaft und Wunder im Wirken Jesu," *Der historische Jesus und der kerygmatische Christus* (Berlin, 1960) 389–402 (397).

III SIGNIFICANCE AND FUNCTION OF THE MIRACLES OF JESUS

1. For further details see F. Mussner, "Die Bedeutung von Mk 1:14f für die Reichsgottesverkündigung Jesu," *TThZ* 66 (1957) 257–275.

2. J. Schmid, *Das Evangelium nach Markus* (Regensburg, 1954) 45. See also W. Grundmann, *Das Evangelium nach Lukas,* 238: "The exorcisms of Jesus belong in the hour of the coming fulfillment of the reign of God. . . ."

3. See G. Delling, *"Botschaft und Wunder im Wirken Jesu," Der historische Jesus und der kerygmatische Christus* (Berlin, 1960) 389–402.

4. See also R. Schnackenburg, *God's Rule and*

Kingdom (New York, 1963) 114–159; specifically for Luke see G. Voss, *Die Christologie der lukanischen Schriften in Grundzügen* (Paris-Brussels, 1965) 25–39 ("Das Wirken Jesu als Offenbarung der Gottesherrschaft").

5. W. Grundmann, *Das Evangelium nach Markus,* 39.

6. See J. Becker, *Das Heil Gottes* ("Studien zur Umwelt des NT," 3 [Göttingen, 1964]) 199–215; F. W. Maier, *Jesus, Lehrer der Gottesherrschaft* (Würzburg, 1965) 85–90 (86: "The reign of God is already in the air, it announces itself, it is taking over—in one word, it attacks. Though it is an entirely extraterrestrial, transcendent, heavenly category, it makes itself, nevertheless, already felt as a very vitalizing, active, warlike-offensive force, as a trailblazing, helping, and ultimately morally advancing power as well.").

7. Becker, *op. cit.* 202. Concerning form-criticism and the historical question see above all H. Schürmann, "Mt 10:5b–6 und die Vorgeschichte des synoptischen Aussendungsberichtes," *Neutestamentliche Aufsätze* (Festschrift für J. Schmid) (Regensburg, 1963) 270–282. According to Schürmann "an old piece of narrative becomes visible" in the account of the mission "which relates a great messianic deed of Jesus on account of Israel. Jesus' 'mission' of the disciples is reported in

the fashion of a major attack on Israel, which once again is to face the messianic decision" (280). This "major attack" is connected with the proclamation of the proximity of the kingdom of God, which would include the salvation of Israel.

8. Mark 5:1–20=Matt 8:28–34=Luke 8:26–39. For a comprehensive discussion of the problematic character of this miracle of Jesus see A. Vögtle, "Die historische und theologische Tragweite der heutigen Evangelienforschung," *ZKTh* 86 (1964) 385–417 (399–402).

9. W. Grundmann, *Das Evangelium nach Markus,* 110.

10. The direct command of Jesus to the wind and the sea which is the "core" in Mark is missing in Matthew and Luke (G. Bornkamm); in this way the process is already "de-demonized" considerably, though not really for the best of it, because thereby the opposing demonic forces are no more shown in all their viciousness. See G. Bornkamm, "Die Sturmstillung im Matthäus-Evangelium," *Überlieferung und Auslegung im Matthäus-Evangelium* (Neukirchen, 1960) 48–53.

11. One can classify the miracles of Jesus into several categories, such as healing miracles, nature miracles, expulsions of demons, and

resurrections. It would be wrong, however, to attempt a critical selection from these categories and accept, for instance, only the healings as genuine miracles of Jesus. These categories form a unified whole in which the *universal horizon* of the eschatological kingdom of God manifests itself. For that reason a critical limitation of the miracle-working of Jesus to one group only treats the synoptic understanding of the kingdom of God from a one-sided point of view. Rather, the categories of miracles are different facets of a unified whole.

12. See J. B. Metz, "Caro cardo salutis," *Hochland* 55 (1962) 97–107.

13. *RGG* ³VI, 1837.

14. The dualistic cosmic battle situations, too, which form the background to the Christological kerygma in the prison letters, particularly in the letter to the Colossians, are anticipated in the concept that the kingdom of God forms the antipole to the reign of Satan (see J. Becker, *Das Heil Gottes*, 212).

15. H. Schürmann, *LThK* ²VI, 123.

16. "All those major miracles designated as σημεῖα force our attention on him who works them. At the same time they make the authority and saving power transparent which was bestowed on him" (R. Schnackenburg, *Das Johannesevangelium, I. Teil* [Freiburg,

1965] 352, particularly 344–356 [Excursus: Die johanneischen 'Zeichen' ”]); see S. Hofbeck, Σημεῖον (Münsterschwarzach, 1966).

17. See F. Mussner, *Die johanneische Sehweise und die Frage nach dem historischen Jesus* (“Quaestiones Disputatae,” 27 [Freiburg, 1965]).

18. It is possible that the fourth evangelist made use of a “σημεῖα-source” in his “sign” accounts, “from which he only selected a limited number. These few σημεῖα, however, he analyzed on the basis of their deeper Christological meaning. For that reason, they are partly much more detailed in order to insure their reality and unassailability and to bring to light their entire meaning” (R. Schnackenburg, *Das Johannesevangelium, I. Teil,* 54 [see specifically 51–54]).

IV THE FORM-CRITICAL QUESTION: THE MIRACLES OF JESUS IN THE TRADITION OF THE GOSPELS

1. Mark 6:47–56; Matt 14:22–33; John 6:16–21.
2. E. Haenchen, *Der Weg Jesu. Eine Erklärung des Markus-Evangeliums und der kanonischen Parallelen* Berlin, (1966) 251.
3. See Mark 4:13, 40; 5:31; 8:4, 17 ff; 9:11, 18 f, 32, 34; 10:13, 25 ff.
4. See H. Zimmermann, “Das absolute ‘Ich bin’

in der Redeweise Jesu," *TThZ* 69 (1960) 1–20 (12 f).

5. Haenchen, *op cit.* 252 ff. Haenchen lists among others the following observations and questions: "Why does Jesus urge and even force the disciples to leave without Him?" "Why should the disciples not stay until he dismissed the crowds?" "If we try to get a descriptive picture of the event, then we are running short of time." "Shall all these 5000 people go away . . . in the dark? How are they to find . . . farms and villages where they will be able to spend the night?" And why does Jesus at first want to pass his disciples by (see Mark 6:48), whereas he does, indeed, intend to help them?

6. Haenchen, *op. cit.* 255: "What is said here about the feeding and the walk on the sea (whereby Jesus reveals his divine power) describes, not events from Jesus' life on earth, but the kind which faith later ascribed to Him."

7. *Ibid.*

8. See F. Mussner, "Der 'historische' Jesus," *TThZ* 69 (1960) 321–337.

9. See J. Blank, "Die johanneische Brotrede," *Bibel und Leben* 7 (1966) 193–207 (206 f). The misunderstanding of the disciples symbolizes the misunderstanding of the people of Israel vis-à-vis Jesus. Everything remains

enigmatic. Misunderstanding is replaced by understanding only when the "anonymity" of Jesus, to which particularly his passion (the cross) belong, can be seen faithfully together with the glorification through his resurrection and elevation. It is exactly this unbelieving astonishment which the "believing confessor, in accordance with Mark, recognizes as an indication of Jesus and his messianic mission" (U. Lutz, "Das Geheimnismotiv und die markinische Christologie," ZNW [1965] 9–30 [29]). Thus, the situation which Israel was in, vis-à-vis the pre-Easter Jesus, is apparently indicated in the misunderstanding of the disciples. That is why this misunderstanding corresponds basically to the historical situation, even though Mark made consistent and conscious use of this misunderstanding motif in his treatment of the evangelical tradition.

10. One would possibly consider the account of Jesus' walk on the sea as an "Easter story" which was subsequently moved back into the pre-Easter life of Jesus. Yet there is not too much to be gained. Rather, the account in Mark becomes even more unintelligible.

11. A further development of the understanding of the miracle tradition in Matthew is to be found particularly in H. J. Held, "Matthäus

als Interpret der Wundergeschichten," *Überlieferung und Auslegung im Matthäusevangelium* ("Wissenschaftliche Monographien
zum AT und NT," 1 [Neukirchen, 1960])
155–287. See also F. Kamphaus, "Die Wun-
derberichte der Evangelien," *Bibel und Leben* 6 (1965) 122–135.

v FAITH AND THE MIRACLES OF JESUS

1. G. Bornkamm, *Jesus von Nazareth* (Stuttgart, 1956) 121.
2. See A. Vögtle, "Der Spruch vom Jonaszei-
chen," *Synoptische Studien (Festschrift für
A. Wikenhauser)* (Freiburg, 1953) 230–277.
Translator's note: The "sign of Jonah" is
the resurrection of Jesus (Matt 12:39; 16:4;
Luke 11:29).
3. See G. Söhngen, "Wunderzeichen und
Glaube," *Die Einheit in der Theologie* (Munich, 1952) 265–285.
4. Concerning the topic faith and miracle see
above all H. J. Held, "Matthäus als Interpret der Wundergeschichten," *Überlieferung
und Auslegung im Matthäusevangelium*
("Wissenschaftliche Monographien zum AT
und NT," 1 [Neukirchen, 1960]) 263–284,
who offers important insights with respect
to Matthew.

VI THE MIRACLES OF JESUS AND
THE HOPE OF THE WORLD

1. J. B. Metz, *LThK* ²X, 1264.
2. *Ibid.* 1264 f.
3. E. Peterson, "Was ist der Mensch?" *Theologische Traktate* (Munich, 1951) 227–238 (227).
4. See H. Schlier, *Mächte und Gewalten im Neuen Testament* ("Quaestiones disputatae," 3 [Freiburg, 1958]); in English, Schlier, *Principalities and Powers in the New Testament* (New York, 1961).
5. H. Schlier, "Über die Hoffnung," *Besinnung auf das Neue Testament* (Freiburg, 1964) 134–145 (139).
6. See K. Rahner, "Weltgeschichte und Heilsgeschichte," *Schriften zur Theologie* V (Einsiedeln, 1962) 115–135 (115).
7. J. B. Metz, *LThK* ²X, 1265.

VII THE MIRACLES OF JESUS AND THE
"DEMYTHOLOGIZATION" OF THE NEW TESTAMENT

1. See for instance R. Paret, *Mohammed und der Koran* ("Urban Bücherei," 32 [Stuttgart, 1957]) 63 ff, 87 ff.
2. My pupil A. Polag will elaborate on this point in more detail in a thesis on the Christology of the logia sources.

3. Compare especially F. Vonessen, *Mythos und Wahrheit. Bultmanns "Entmythologisierung" und die Philosophie der Mythologie* (Einsiedeln, 1964). This work is perhaps the best criticism of Bultmann's demythologization program. Every person who reads it should study it thoroughly.

4. *Retractationes* I:13,3.